BawB's Raven Feathers
Reflections on the simple things in life

VOLUME V

Robert Chomany

INVERMERE PRESS • CALGARY, CANADA

Copyright © 2015, Robert Chomany

All rights reserved. No part of this publication may be reproduced or transmitted in any form or by any means, electronic or mechanical, including photocopying, recording, or any information storage and retrieval system without permission in writing from the author.

ISBN 978-0-9918821-9-9 (v. 5 : softcover)

Illustration: Jessee Wise
Book Design: Fiona Raven Book Design
Chief Editor: Rachel Small, Faultless Finish Editing
Proofreader: Carrie Mumford

Published by
Robert Chomany
Calgary, Alberta, Canada
bchomany@telusplanet.net

Printed in the United States of America

www.bawbsravenfeathers.net

This series of books is dedicated to my mom—without her love, patience and guidance I would not be the man I am today. She taught me to appreciate compassion, to stand alone, and to be proud of who I am, and she gave me strength to pursue my dreams.

Take on the world because you can,
and enjoy your every mile;
it's contagious you know, enjoying life,
so share your biggest smile.

Let Go

Do you need to let go of something? A feeling? A nagging "what if"? How many times in your day do you hear "let it go"? How many times do you wish you hadn't heard it? It's tough for those outside your personal space to understand the situations with which you are faced, and it's tougher for them to understand what effects the situations are having on you. Letting go of something may be easy for one person but devastating for another. This is why it's important to ask yourself what you're holding on to needlessly. No one else can tell you.

Letting go is not a natural response but a learned one, I believe, and unfortunately those who tell us to "let go" will often desire only to see us "move on" and "be happy." Frequently though, the effects of an action need to be embraced. If there is a lesson it must be learned. If an action caused a feeling within you, then that feeling should be acknowledged. It is possible to immediately let go of the action, and to forgive, but letting go of the feeling it caused is not so easy—and sometimes not even possible. But with strength, one can let go of the energy attached to a feeling, and this in turn will bring peace.

Along with the big things, there will be many little things you cannot control: bad drivers, cold coffee, missing a favorite show, etc. These little things can build up easily and quickly, and may make you wonder why you feel so stressed out, but they won't leave you with lasting feelings. So though they may rile you up, you can find the strength to "let them go" if you so choose.

> Breathe in the good air, let go of the bad;
> your life is composed of the choices you've had.

Are you prepared each day for what life brings,
or do you wait with bated breath?
Are you calm enough to let things slide,
or do they turn into life and death?
It's so much easier to just put on a smile
and accept what we cannot control.
Life is short, but when the days seem long,
it's better to let things roll.

It never helps to get upset:
just look for another view.
Take a breath then find your calm,
and be happy being you.

With each new day comes the sense of
not knowing what waits in store for you;
so many things will need to be done,
and there's so much living to do.
Just close the door to negative energy
and leave it far behind,
then build a new door with positive thoughts
and happiness you will find.

Believe in you and choose to feel
that wherever you are, you belong;
surround yourself with positive energy,
and feel your soul get strong.

Learn to let go and believe in yourself,
find balance and take care of you.
You were born in this world to be happy,
and to have fun in all that you do.

There are two ways to look at life today:
one sky will have sunshine and one will be grey.
If you choose to smile right off the bat,
your skies will be cloudless and blue,
when you focus on darkness and wallow in gloom,
it's hard to change the view.

If you refuse to let go
of what's weighing you down,
then it will continue to be
the reason you frown.

The cure for stress is to let things go,
don't pack your troubles around;
the dangerous thing about worry is that
it might become profound.
Share your smile, try not to worry,
and brush the stress away.
Have fun being you in all that you do,
and enjoy what comes your way.

Relax your grip on the golden ring
and share instead a smile.
Remember the happiness that tranquility brings
and enjoy it for a while.

Sometimes it's tough to know where to go
when your heart feels broken in two,
but try if you can to focus on balance:
let your mind be a part of life too.
Breathe with a purpose and remember the balance
between heart and mind and soul;
focus on you being happy with you,
and let life simply unfold.

With age comes wisdom, and knowledge to share:
one important life lesson is "don't poke the bear."
Let things be, in time they will pass;
be real and just understand,
when people are down or a little bit off,
it could be they might need a hand.

The path you're on could change tomorrow,
it's different with every mile;
no worries my friend, just go with the flow,
and put on your biggest smile.

Journey

A journey is a desire to become, a need to complete, and a yearning to appreciate. A journey is a lifetime filled with moments you remember, good and bad: memories of smiles and bruises, peaks and valleys. A journey can be as simple as a trip to the mailbox. Next time, instead of focusing on the mailbox, notice every step, and the things you have walked past a million times but not seen.

A journey can also be an adventure—have you been there before? Do you know the way? If you've been there once or twice, can you change your route? And what if you get lost? Is that part of your adventure? Have you ever taken a journey somewhere because it feels like your destiny? The journey itself is a milestone, a time to be filled with wonder and learning, to explore both your surroundings and your inner self.

There is also the spiritual journey. The soul drives during this one, and it requires belief in yourself and a desire to BE outside of your self. If you will, think of your physical body as a vessel in which your mind and soul travel. Occasionally you may wish to travel light and leave the vessel behind—this is possible and very pleasing. Travelling without the vessel becomes a journey with no beginning and no end. It becomes an experience of being where you are not. Your mind travels without the vessel when you think of someone special and then see his or her face wearing the smile you sent a second ago in the wind.

We each have journeys to take, some solo, some with friends. We each have places to be. We each have our own destinies. To get to where we are going is, of course, the objective, but the time it takes to get there is what comprises the journey. Your journey, your life, is what it is because you make it that way.

> Enjoy each and every step you take,
> for others will follow the footprints you make.

Consult the map within your thoughts
and pick a direction to go;
whatever you do is up to you—
it's time to get on with the show.

One step forward, no steps back,
it's the way that you should travel.
Whatever direction you've pointed your mind
is the way life will unravel.

Take that first step and start your journey
in any direction you choose;
as long as you're moving and have aspirations
you're never going to lose.

You will often have choices of roads up ahead,
all of them different and new,
but you can't go wrong if you choose the road
that is always best suited for YOU.

The morning sun will show itself—
it's your choice now to look.
Your life unfolds, it's in your hands:
it's your pen that writes your book.
Smile wide as you follow your path,
don't live with expectation.
Be happy being you today
and create your own elation.

The footprints you leave are yours from the start.
The direction you travel is what sets you apart.

You'll get there you know, one step at a time,
and you may come upon a bridge or two;
the bridges are there to span a challenge
and to help make it easier for you.
You're not being timed, you cross when you like,
it's a choice for you to make,
so rely on the mettle you have in your soul,
and choose things for your own sake.

Live in today, walk the path you are on
and watch where you are going.
Keep your chin up high as you amble,
so your smile is always showing.
This is your life, this is your journey,
to wherever it shall lead;
now walk it with your head held high
because your soul is free.

How high could you truly fly

if you really stretched your wings?

Would you make it to the furthest cloud,

where the wind begins to sing?

This life you live, the path you're on,

is the only chance you've got,

so it might be time to enjoy those things

that in the past you've sought.

"No" is something you hear each day,
and depending on how it is said,
it can be a line drawn in the sand,
or it can be a door instead.
You're on a path with twists and turns,
with lots of chances to grow,
so if you don't like the direction you're going,
you too have the voice to say "no."

Adventures can happen to you every day,
when you're right here at home or while you're away.

Everywhere you walk today,

every step and every mile,

choose to see something that stays with you

and attach it to a smile.

Direction is just the way that you look
to find the quickest way there,
but the beauty of not having a map
is the joy of the journey you share.

So you're on a path and you're unsure
of where it's going to go,
but sometimes life is full of adventure
and you don't have to know.
Open your eyes and see the world,
all the wonders it has to share,
enjoy the moments one at a time—
you'll know when you are there.

Be Present

Being present means being here: wherever "here" is. With our communication technology, being present doesn't have to involve a physical presence anymore. One can Skype to a room and be present. Being present means being part of the universal energy flow, present and alive in your own way. Being present can also involve offering to help, recognizing moments that require a response, being part of someone else's life, and being able to present yourself accordingly in situations. Presence is not just being there in the room; presence is taking part in the actions occurring in the room; presence is taking note of what you do or say, of how you react, and of how you feel.

I believe it is most important to be present when standing in front of a mirror. Truly see who is standing there in front of you, and know who that person is. Be a part of the life that you see. There will be moments when you might think it easier to just dissociate yourself from yourself, but you will still be there—you will still be present in the moment. With practice, it becomes easier to accept these moments as simply a part of being present.

When you find yourself present and accounted for in today, take stock of your feelings. Are you happy? Are you wearing a smile? Are you glad to be here? You have the ability to change everything about your presence, from the simplistic, such as your clothes or makeup, to the more advanced, such as your energy and smile. You have not been invited to take part in this life; rather, it was a gift given to you to enjoy, to be present in, so relax and breathe. By yourself or in a crowd, be yourself, be present in the moment, feel the energy of simply being, and present yourself to the universe as light and well-being.

Don't wait for that special time, don't think of those perfect words to say: just be you and be happy. Walk in the rain, go out for dinner, send flowers because it's Tuesday, be present in today and live because you can—because you are "here."

Take that step to where you are going, and take it in today.
Be present with a smile that shows because it is your way.

On your way to wherever you're going
be sure to take a minute,
to appreciate this beautiful world
and everything that's in it:
the flowers and trees, the grass and the bees,
the brook that flows with laughter.
Enjoy the sun whenever it shines,
and if it rains, then the rainbow after.

Sometimes something will catch your attention
in a world full of beautiful things,
like the intricate colors of a single flower,
or the melody a little bird sings.
Walk your path that lies ahead
with a calm and balanced stride,
while taking in all that your senses will share
and feeling good from inside.

Choose to live each moment today—
tomorrow will come anew.
Yesterday is a memory
and because of it you grew.

Wherever you are, whatever you're doing,
every moment in life is new;
if you choose to be happy in every moment,
then life will be good to you.

Life is for living and enjoying yourself
with each new challenge that mounts,
and life is for giving yourself a chance
to make all of your moments count.

Step on, step up, get into the groove,
spread your wings and fly;
life will happen, ready or not,
don't let it pass you by.
Don't waste your moments making plans
then hope that they transpire—
instead turn up the sound of the drums
and dance around life's fire.

Live your best from where you stand,
in the very moment you're there,
for in the blink of an eye things could change,
and catch you unaware.

Sadly it seems we just get too busy
to remember to look out for ourselves;
before you know it the time is all gone,
and memories are stacked on the shelves.
Swallow hard and take a breath,
feel the wind and spread your wings.
Take the time to smile at life
and see what your happiness brings.

Find a moment to relax whenever you can,
enjoy the balance of being.
Don't just look at what is there,
but savor the beauty you're seeing.

Yesterday's footsteps echo behind you
as you move forward through today,
and tomorrow looms within your sight,
but here and now you'll stay.

You'll see that tomorrow will come and go,
and such little time it takes,
so enjoy each minute that passes by
and smile for your own sake.

"In a minute," we say, we'll get it done,
in a minute we realize we're late;
in a minute a day of our life has passed,
now a minute we'll have to wait.
Too much time we waste just catching up
because we think we're behind,
but if you stop moving for just one breath,
it's amazing what you will find.
In a minute it's clear our time is contained
in whatever it is we're doing,
and if we take time to enjoy our lives,
each minute becomes worth viewing.

Feel the wind in your hair
and the sun on your face:
you belong in this moment
in this very place.

Learn

Life without learning is but a collection of minutes with no meaning. Since the beginning of recorded time and long before, life has been filled with learning. All life, all living things, learn. Did you know that now "they" are creating computers that "learn"— machines that think? When are we going to learn that our existence as a species is enhanced by our ability to think for ourselves? Do we really need computers to do our thinking and learning for us?

I think it's fascinating to watch nature, to see how she helps all living beings learn. For example, a honeybee after returning to the hive must go through a series of motions, a dance if you will, to explain to its fellow bees where the field of flowers is. Do you remember how you learned how to communicate the simplest of tasks to a fellow human being?

Personally, I never want to and never will stop learning. I enjoy not just learning things, but also learning how to learn. I came from an old-school education system, through which I increased my knowledge by reading books. Now, I share my knowledge by writing them. I learned about myself by being myself, by experiencing things firsthand, by watching others, by asking questions. I learned how to be comfortable learning how to be a better me.

Learning should never be viewed as a task but as a gift. There is so much diversity in the world, so many cultures, so many billions of people all with unique thoughts and ideas. Can you imagine how much energy is out there bundled up in thoughts? How much potential we have to teach and learn from each other? Life is but a series of moments, and each moment presents an opportunity to experience something new, a chance to learn. Embrace these chances.

Learn by experience, learn because you can.
Learn to be a better you—become your biggest fan.

Look to things you see each day that inspire you to live,
especially the things you see that nature loves to give.

Perhaps your path keeps going in circles
and this has you a little concerned,
you know there's a lesson behind it all
but one you've not yet learned.
In order to grow you need to believe
that where you're going is better,
but always remember that water is water
and it never gets any wetter.

Forward movement, a little each day,
is the way you are going to grow,
and life will be better if you enjoy the walk,
with a smile you love to show.

Life has its moments set up for us
to deal with as we see fitting,
the challenge of course is to grow in the knowledge
that learning is better than quitting.

Keeping life simple is sometimes a chore,
there's always a challenge or two,
so learning the options that help you succeed
is always the best thing for you.

Just when you think you've seen it all,
you're filled with prodigious surprise:
something happened you didn't expect
and you can't believe your eyes.
Could this be what life is about,
all these things that you're still learning?
The knowledge you gain while on your journey
can fill a mind that's yearning.

You won't know what it is you don't know
until you take time to look,
and some of the things you might need to learn
you won't find in any book.
The beauty, strength, and energy of nature
is found while you're living and being,
and the knowledge to gain from the lessons of life
cannot be learned without seeing.

The voice that will guide you throughout your journey
is the voice of experience past;
it comes from the skills and knowledge you gain,
and it offers lessons that last.

Wisdom comes when we live our lives
and learn from what has been;
it comes by quietly listening to what's said,
and appreciating what is seen.

Stand up and breathe then go for a walk,
be proud of what you have sought.
Build on the knowledge you already have
and do things that others have not.

Life is about all the new things you learn,
added to the things you know;
it's about the sparkle in your eyes
that enhances the smile you show.
Life is about the things that are real
and not the way that things seem;
life is for sharing and caring and giving,
and finally living your dreams.

Dream

Do you remember your dreams? Do you dream while you are awake? Dreaming can often be an escape from a stressful reality, and it can take place in a moment you wish you were somewhere else, or somebody else. Dreams, wishes, and imagination are all based on things that we believe will add intrigue to the moment, or our lives.

It is healthy to dream? I believe dreaming is part of a normal existence. We learn how when we are kids—not how to dream but rather, of what to dream. We imagine ourselves as superheroes flying through the air, we wish for things that will make us happy, and we dream of places we would like to be. Now that you are older, can you honestly say that anything has changed? Do you still imagine, wish, and dream? Have you even become better at it?

The really nice thing about dreams is that they often enhance who we are by simply putting smiles on our faces or helping us create goals to aim for. Our dreams can become our attainable possibilities, or portals to different or more desirable ways of life. Our dreams can also be of others, of seeing them in better places or watching them achieve what they desire.

Remember though, your feet are on the ground. Lose yourself in your dreams every now and then and shoot for the moon, but come back to earth to share your smile and be present. Then enjoy the next moment you decide to dream, and be present in that space too.

> Dream of the things that are just out of reach—
> your heart will be happy that your mind it can teach.

Point your mind towards a lofty dream,
spread your wings and fly;
the wind will hold you while you soar
in a peaceful azure sky.

Believe in you then watch what happens
in the dreams that you create:
the hills you climb will level out,
and your path ahead is straight.

What does "inspire" mean to you—
is it something you do without thinking?
If others are down can you put on a smile
and possibly keep them from sinking?
And what about you, what's your inspiration?
Can you see it when you look in the mirror?
Can you smile at you as you do what you do,
while your dreams bring happiness nearer?

There is no room for doubt in your life,
you need to be focused on you;
whatever your goals, believe to achieve,
and succeed in all that you do.

Reach for the sky with negative thinking
and you won't get very far,
but fill your mind with positive thoughts
and you can touch the stars.

Smile today because you can and you're happy being you;
be present in what brings you joy, and keep your dreams in view.

Let today be the day to dream in wonder
of what the future may hold,
let today be the day to set aside
all the disparaging things you're told.
What the future brings is up to you,
so simply make some choices;
choose to do what's right for you
and don't listen to negative voices.

Relax your grip on reality
and pause for a moment or two.
Can you breathe a little easier?
Have you changed your point of view?
Change the way you look at things,
add some abstract to your real—
it can change your whole perspective,
and alter how you feel.

Believe in your thoughts, and in what you can do,
believe in your dreams and make them come true.
Step out from the doldrums and open your wings,
feel the wind in your soul and the change that it brings.

Change

Change is good, change is inevitable, change is commensurate with effort and expectation. We often get bored with life and begin to take things for granted, and when we do so, change does not easily occur. However, if we are excited about what we are doing and recognize potential for growth, then we will welcome change. Quite simply, life is change: change in who we are and how we look, change in our environment, and of course, change in our perception.

Our views, however rosy they may be, constantly change, with breaking news or others' opinions. And the changes right in front of us, like a new parking lot over a once-grassy park, can change the way we think about things. Some folks need change to be gradual, and some need time to cope with the difference between what was and what will be. Perhaps you can change the way you think in an instant, or perhaps you need a "sleep on it" period. You might reject change and adapt to a situation based on stubbornness. But any way you look at it, change is going to happen. How you react to it is up to you.

It is your choice to accept or deny a change after thinking it through. It's not about right or wrong, it's about the benefits or setbacks of change, and the action/reaction principle. And there is no time limit. You can change your mind whenever you like, and when you do, if you were wrong, admit it. If you were right, move forward without falling prey to the "I told you so" moment; instead, be glad you made the right decision and pat your own back.

Change the things you can control if you wish, and adapt to the things you cannot. Roll with the changes, go with the flow, change up your smile with each new outfit you throw on. If you have nothing to smile about when you change, then smile because you are changing. Keep your heart flexible enough to accept the changes of life, keep your soul open enough to accept the changes in your spirit, and keep your mind nimble enough to work with the changes around you.

> Where you were a minute ago
> is different from where you are now;
> where you are going may change tomorrow,
> but you'll make it through somehow.

Destiny is flexible,
it's not always carved in stone:
your future is designed by you,
and often by you alone.
The choices you decide to make
and the changes that will ensue,
are directly connected to your own thoughts,
and to your point of view.

You can change who you are today
by simply making a choice;
you can find yourself within your soul
by listening to your own voice.

Your life will change each passing day,
so make the time worthwhile.
Wherever you are just being you,
make sure you're you with a smile.

Sometimes we have to reflect on ourselves,
and decide if revisions are due,
so don't be afraid to peruse your options
then choose what works for you.

Feelings can sometimes get in the way,
emotions have no filter,
and often how you think about things
can set you slightly off-kilter.
No need to panic just welcome the changes,
let nature take its course.
Deal with the glitches as calm as you can—
you'll never win using force.

You don't always have to follow a course
just to stay in the norm;
keep doing what you do, just being you,
but try to change up your form.

Don't hesitate when opportunity knocks
as it may not come again,
and sometimes the best way to keep moving forward
is to work along the grain.
Plan the steps to where you're going,
and don't take this chance for granted;
if you have an idea to better yourself,
then water that seed once it's planted.

Don't be afraid to take that first step
and make your life happen today.
Take control of your decisions
and listen to what fate has to say.

Life will change from day to day, be it destiny or fate;
the way you choose to deal with things is the life that you create.

There should be no stress if you want to be happy;
your burden should always be light.
Enjoy where you are and the things that you have,
but always keep changes in sight.

The warmth of spring will take its time
to reveal the earth we know;
the ice breaks up then melts away
and calm water starts to show.
Truth be known we're much the same,
we have thoughts we try to hide,
but when springtime comes we should feel the wind
and warm our hearts inside.

One chapter ends and a new one begins,
change can take place without warning;
sunsets are beautiful and draw your gaze,
but there's something intriguing about morning.
With each new day embrace not knowing
what may be in store for you—
so many things that can be done,
and so much living to do.

Let go of the anchors that slow your journey,
be present with positive thought;
change your mind and learn from your dreams,
then give life all you've got.

Acknowledgments

I would like to thank the people in my life who have been there to help me along this new and uncharted path on which I walk.

Rachel Small - Editor, Faultless Finish Editing
Carrie Mumford - Proofreader
Jessee Wise - Illustrator
Fiona Raven - Designer

And to the souls in my life who have given me strength, support and inspiration, this adventure would not have happened without you all. Special thanks to all those who share my path, my life and my smiles.

About the Author

Robert (BawB) Chomany is the author of the BawB's Raven Feathers series, pure and simple inspirational books. He was born in Calgary, Alberta, with a clear view of the mountains to the west. These mountains eventually drew Bob in, and he spent many years living in the company of nature, exploring his spiritual side.

Bob pursues his many interests with passion. You are just as likely to find him twisting a wrench, or riding his motorcycle, as you are to find him holding a pen, writing.

Bob still lives in Calgary, where he finds happiness by simply living with a smile and sharing his words of wisdom with others.

Made in the USA
Charleston, SC
20 February 2017